Robert Fulton

by Lola M. Schaefer

Consulting Editor: Gail Saunders-Smith, Ph.D.

Consultant: Dr. Martin C. Striegel
Historian and Curator
Howard Steamboat Museum
Jeffersonville, Indiana

Pebble Books

an imprint of Capstone Press
Mankato, Minnesota

Pebble Books are published by Capstone Press
151 Good Counsel Drive, P.O. Box 669, Mankato, Minnesota 56002
http://www.capstone-press.com

1 2 3 4 5 6 05 04 03 02 01 00

Library of Congress Cataloging-in-Publication Data
Schaefer, Lola M., 1950–
    Robert Fulton/by Lola M. Schaefer.
    p. cm.—(Famous people in transportation)
    Includes bibliographical references and index.
    Summary: Simple text and photographs present the life of Robert Fulton and his
contributions to transportation.
    ISBN 0-7368-0547-8
    1. Fulton, Robert, 1765–1815—Juvenile literature. 2. Marine engineers—United
States—Biography—Juvenile literature. [1. Fulton, Robert, 1765–1815. 2. Inventors.
3. Steamboats—History.] I. Title. II. Series.
VM140.F9 S33   2000
623.8′24′092—dc21
[B]
                                       99-047367

Note to Parents and Teachers

The series Famous People in Transportation supports national social studies standards related to the ways technology has changed people's lives. This book describes the life of Robert Fulton and illustrates his contributions to transportation. The photographs support early readers in understanding the text. This book also introduces early readers to subject-specific vocabulary words, which are defined in the Words to Know section. Early readers may need assistance to read some words and to use the Table of Contents, Words to Know, Read More, Internet Sites, and Index/Word List sections of the book.

Table of Contents

4

Robert Fulton was born in 1765. He grew up in Pennsylvania. Robert had many skills. He liked to draw and to experiment with machines.

6

Robert began to work for a silversmith when he was about 16 years old. He made jewelry. Later, he opened a shop. He painted pictures of people in the shop.

8

Robert moved to England in 1786. He worked as an artist there. He also invented a machine that cut and polished marble. People used the marble to make furniture and other goods.

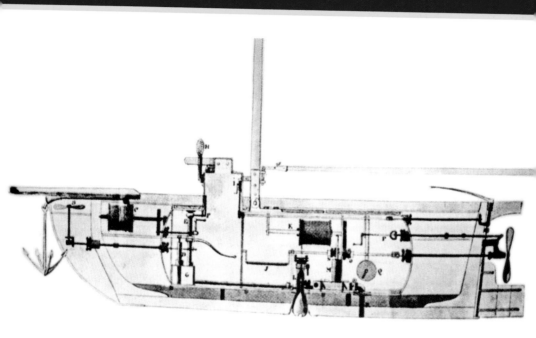

Robert moved to France in 1797. There he invented a type of submarine. He called it the *Nautilus.*

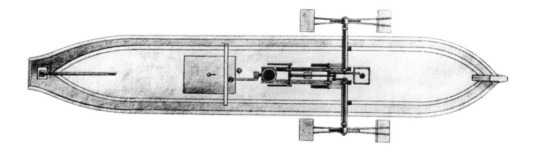

Robert made plans for a type of steamboat. In 1803, he steered the steamboat down the Seine River in France. The steamboat traveled 4 miles (6 kilometers) per hour.

Robert returned to the United States in 1806. He built steamboats that were faster and longer. These boats carried people and goods on New York's rivers.

Robert's steamboats followed schedules. People could plan when they wanted to travel. Travelers could depend on Robert's steamboats.

Americans liked to travel on steamboats. They wanted to travel on other rivers. Robert planned and built new steamboats to travel on the Mississippi River.

20

Robert Fulton died in 1815. He had invented ways to use steam engines on boats. His inventions made travel easier.

Words to Know

experiment—to plan to try something new

invention—a new idea or machine; someone may create an invention after studying a problem and experimenting with solutions; John Fitch invented the first steamboat in 1787.

marble—a hard stone that has colored patterns; people use marble in furniture, buildings, and statues.

schedule—a plan of times and places; Fulton's steamboats carried people and goods to places at times that followed a set schedule.

silversmith—someone who makes or fixes silver objects

steamboat—a boat powered by a steam engine; heat from burning coal or wood boils water; the boiling water creates steam that moves parts of the engine; the engine moves the boat.

submarine—a ship that can travel both on the surface of the water and underwater

Read More

Bowen, Andy Russell. *A Head Full of Notions: A Story about Robert Fulton.* Creative Minds. Minneapolis: Carolrhoda Books, 1997.

Flammang, James M. *Robert Fulton: Inventor and Steamboat Builder.* Historical American Biographies. Springfield, N.J.: Enslow Publishers, 1999.

Kroll, Steven. *Robert Fulton: From Submarine to Steamboat.* New York: Holiday House, 1999.

Internet Sites

John Fitch and the Steamboat
http://osage.voorhees.k12.nj.us/FOURTH/LARSEN/ JKIDS/STORIES/page7.htm

Robert Fulton
http://xroads.virginia.edu/~HYPER/DETOC/ transport/fulton.html

Steamboat Learning Center
http://www.steamboats.com/classroom.html

Index/Word List

Word Count: 222
Early-Intervention Level: 17

Editorial Credits
Martha E. H. Rustad, editor; Kia Bielke, cover designer; Kimberly Danger, photo researcher

Photo Credits
Archive Photos, 4, 6, 14
Corbis-Bettmann, 10, 12, 18
FPG International LLC, cover inset
Independence National Historical Park, cover
North Wind Picture Archives, 1, 8, 16, 20